Arctic Adventure

INUIT LIFE IN THE 1800S

ODYSSEY

SMITHSONIAN INSTITUTION

For Pat and Geo and their adventurous move to the north. —D.R.

To Terry, my loving husband. —P.M.

Soundprints is a division of Trudy Corporation, Norwalk, Connecticut.

Book design: Alleycat Design Inc. New York, NY

First Edition
10 9 8 7 6 5 4 3 2 1
Printed in Hong Kong

Library of Congress Cataloging-in-Publication Data

Rau, Dana Meachen, 1971–
        Arctic adventure: Inuit life in the 1800s/by Dana Rau;
    illustrated by Peg Magovern
            p.   cm.
        Summary: While visiting the exhibit on native cultures at the National Museum of Natural History, Tomas travels back in time and becomes an Inuit boy living in the Arctic regions in the 1800s.
        ISBN 1-56899-416-8 (hardcover)   ISBN 1-56899-417-6 (softcover)
        1. Inuit—Juvenile fiction. [1. Inuit—Fiction. 2. Eskimos—Fiction.
3. Arctic regions—Fiction. 4. Time travel—Fiction. 5. National Museum of Natural History (U.S.)—Fiction.]
I. Magovern, Peg, ill. II. Title.
PZ7. R193975Ar 1997
[E]—dc21   97-10792
                                                                      CIP
                                                                      AC

Arctic Adventure

INUIT LIFE IN THE 1800S

Written by Dana Meachen Rau
Illustrated by Peg Magovern

Soundprints
Where Children Discover...

Tomas hurries through the center rotunda of the National Museum of Natural History.

"Wait up!" Lucy yells from behind.

"But I've been waiting all day!" Tomas shouts back annoyed. "It's time to see the exhibit I want to see."

Tomas has been patient. He waited while Kevin blabbered on about the blue whale hanging from the ceiling. He followed Lucy through the rooms of gems. And he sat on a bench while Emma stared at the spiders.

Now Tomas wants to see the "Native Cultures of the Americas" exhibit. His scout troop is planning a camping trip and he is curious about people who survived the harsh conditions of the outdoors everyday!

When Tomas enters the exhibit, he stops at the first display and chuckles. It shows an Inuit family laughing at the small seal their son has caught. *They look so real behind the glass!* Tomas thinks.

"Polar Eskimo" he reads on the wall. "The Northernmost People of the World."

Tomas has camped in the autumn before, when the temperature was almost freezing at night. But the Arctic is one of the coldest places on Earth!

How could people survive? he wonders. *It would be too cold for me!*

A cold chill runs down Tomas' spine.

"Wait for us!" Tomas hears voices from behind again. But the voices don't sound like Kevin, Emma, or Lucy! As he turns away from the exhibit he finds he is no longer at the museum! Tomas is outside, the sky is dark, there is nothing but snow as far as he can see, and it is freezing!

Suddenly, three Eskimo children—two boys and one girl—surround him. They are dressed just like the statues in the exhibit.

The land is covered with snow. It looks like a desert, but it's not hot! The cold air—60 degrees below zero—bites Tomas's face, but the rest of his body is comfortable, dressed in a furry parka with a hood, and wearing boots strapped to snowshoes on his feet!

"Are you scared?" the girl asks.

"Why?" He's a little nervous, but he doesn't want her to know.

"For your first hunt tomorrow!" the younger boy blurts excitedly. "I can't wait for the day I go on mine!"

"My first hunt?" Tomas gasps. He doesn't like to hunt. The only shooting he ever does is with his camera, and even that he usually leaves to his friend Lucy!

9

"Aren't the lights beautiful!" The other boy points to the sky.

Tomas looks up. A curtain of flashing lights dances through the stars.

The Northern Lights! Tomas has only seen them once before when his father took his troop camping. His father had said you could see the lights more clearly farther north.

Tomas turns around awkwardly, feeling like a stuffed animal in his coat. Among the snow drifts stands a magnificent structure—an igloo! He recalls from the exhibit that there was only one place where the Inuit built igloos as their shelter all winter long—Canada!

Then Tomas knew where he must be—in the Arctic Circle in the late 1800's, before explorers disturbed the Inuit and their way of life that had existed for four thousand years!

"Come back inside, children! It's time for dinner." A woman waves from the entrance to the igloo.

The three children rush back, and Tomas follows. Even though the igloo is made of snow, it still looks warm and inviting. Four husky dogs nuzzle the children as they run past. Tomas pats one dog's head. "Want to come in and get warm?" Tomas asks.

"You know they can't come inside!" the girl says.

The huskies settle on the snow for the night. "I guess their fur keeps them warm enough," Tomas hopes.

Tomas enters a low, narrow tunnel. He crawls through on his hands and knees. Inside, the igloo opens up into a giant room. The igloo is made of packed snow blocks from the tundra, stacked in circles on top of each other. Air trapped inside the snow acts as insulation. A covering of snow on the outside seals up all the cracks. And as the wind blows, it pushes the house downward, making it as strong as cement.

The tunnel floor is lower than the rest of the igloo. When Tomas steps up to the floor of the room, the air is much warmer. The tunnel floor serves as a cold trap. And because warm air rises, the room is cozy. Only two lamps, burning seal oil, are needed to light the room.

"Akpek, I am running out of oil! I hope our son catches a seal tomorrow!" The woman who had called them in says to a man. Tomas guesses he must be her husband. "I know Mamayauk," the man assures.

They must think I'm part of their family! Tomas realizes. She must be mother, and he must be my father!

In the crowded room, there is another older couple, the three children that met him outside, and an old man bundled in caribou skins in the corner. The parents, aunt, uncle, and the other children (who are either his brothers and sisters, or his cousins) all live together. Tomas figures he must be the oldest son!

There is also the man in the corner. By his age, Tomas guesses he must be the grandfather.

Covering the back half of the igloo is an iglerk—a shelf of snow large enough for the whole family. It is the warmest part of the room. Following the others, Tomas hangs his parka up to dry and beats the snow off his boots with a walrus tusk. Then he climbs onto the caribou hides that cover the iglerk.

For dinner, they eat raw seal meat. Tomas has never eaten seal, or any meat raw! But he doesn't want to say no. Survival is most important. If it were summer, there would be berries to eat. But it is November, the beginning of winter, and if he is going to hunt tomorrow, he needs all his strength. The first bite of seal meat is the worst, but after a while, it doesn't taste so bad. At least he doesn't have to eat his vegetables!

Mamayauk looks concerned while she picks up after dinner. There is not much seal meat left in the storage area. While she cleans, the children play a game. They use a tiny lance to spear a piece of walrus ivory that hangs from the ceiling. Tomas tries, but misses. Akpek gives him a look of disapproval. His aim is not good. How will he ever catch a seal tomorrow?

"Come here, children," the grandfather calls from the corner.

Tomas jumps! This is the first time the old man has spoken. He is going to tell a story. Everyone finds a spot on the iglerk, as if they have all sat for many stories before.

"Ekalukpik, tell us about the polar bear!" one cousin says eagerly.

"Nanuq! The Polar Bear! He is a fierce beast! I hope our son does not meet him tomorrow!" he points a long wrinkled finger at Tomas.

Tomas gulps as Ekalukpik tells of a hunter taken away by an ice floe, who must become a polar bear to swim home. The whole family is mesmerized by his tale.

When he is done, Tomas pleads with him to tell another story.

"No, it is time for rest," the old man says. As the family pulls skins over themselves for added warmth, Ekalukpik motions for Tomas to come closer. He opens Tomas's hand and places something inside it.

"It is a tooth of a great Nanuq," he whispers. "This charm has been in our family for many years. Wear it tomorrow. It will bring you luck."

Once, long ago, Ekalukpik had been a great hunter, too. Tomas doesn't want to let him down.

As Tomas tries to sleep, he thinks about the hunt. For these people it means survival, and from the way everyone is acting, the first hunt is a very special event. He feels honored—and nervous!

Morning arrives and Tomas is ready to go. He wears the charm from Ekalukpik around his neck. Mamayauk helps him into a waterproof parka made of seal intestines! "Yuk!" thinks Tomas, but he knows he would rather be dry than cold and wet from the Beaufort Sea.

Outside the igloo, Akpek harnesses the huskies to a sled made out of pieces of bones and driftwood. As Tomas approaches, the dogs bark eagerly. They seem just as excited as he! He helps Akpek load their kayaks onto the sled.

"Leave space for my big seal," Tomas says confidently.

"Don't worry, son," Akpek pats his son on the back. "We will be pleased with whatever you catch."

But Tomas wants to catch a big seal so his family will have enough meat for the long winter. They climb into the sled and wave to Mamayauk. The huskies carry them to the edge of the ice.

At the water, Tomas and his father climb into their kayaks. They are small boats made of tough sealskin, with a hole in the top for one person.

"How do I . . ." Tomas starts to ask Akpek. But when he looks up, Akpek is already paddling away.

"You take these waters," Akpek shouts back to Tomas as he disappears around an iceberg.

Tomas understands. Akpek cannot stay to help him catch his first seal. Tomas may not be successful, and Mamayauk would be happy if someone came home with a seal. Alone, Tomas scans the water. Cold, dark ripples splash against his boat. He ties the hem of his parka around the rim of the kayak. Now he is completely waterproof!

He paddles out around drifting ice floes. Everything he needs is within reach—his harpoon and spear are attached to the deck of his kayak with straps.

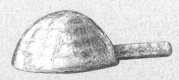

He settles down to wait. He sits for hours. A whale surfaces in the distance and a walrus moans from an ice floe, but he will have to hunt them another day.

Suddenly, Tomas sees a seal pass his boat! It is perfect—huge, fat, and full of blubber. Maybe it's too big. But everyone, especially Ekalukpik, would be impressed.

When the seal swims closer, Tomas hurls his harpoon with all his strength. It strikes the water with a splash and hits the seal!

The seal zips away. The head of the harpoon stays in the seal and pulls a line off his boat. Luckily, Tomas connected the line to a float. The seal, the line, and the float disappear into the water. Now, Tomas just needs to wait for the float to resurface, and he will know where the seal will be coming up next for air.

Tomas waits and waits. But the float is nowhere to be seen. "Maybe the harpoon came loose!" he thinks.

Finally, Tomas sees the float pop up near an ice floe.

He paddles closer, but then stops. A Nanuq is on the ice! The polar bear's white fur blends with the landscape and makes him hard to see.

Tomas is not the only one hunting for seals today!

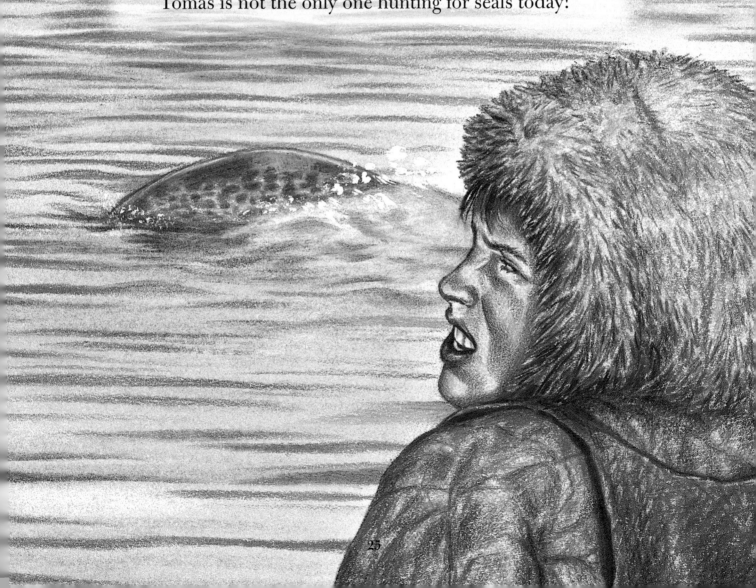

"That polar bear can't take my seal!" Tomas is determined. He doesn't want to go back to the igloo empty handed!

The seal pops his head up out of the water for air. The polar bear swipes with his sharp claws and the seal dives.

"No!" Tomas yells. He clutches the charm around his neck. He feels brave. But as he paddles closer, he changes his mind. The polar bear is huge!

"Growl!" The fierce creature sees Tomas. It is about to jump into the water after the kayak.

"If he flips over my boat, I'll freeze!" Tomas worries.

But the bear suddenly stops and sniffs the air. Its head snaps right, as if it spots something in the water.

With one swipe of its paw it scoops up a seal. It is not Tomas's seal—it is a much smaller one. But it is large enough for the polar bear. He takes it away for an afternoon meal.

Tomas sighs with relief. His seal is still somewhere. Now all that's left is more waiting!

All of the diving and dodging has made the seal tired. Soon, it comes up close to the kayak and Tomas stabs it with a spear. He ties it to his boat, and heads to shore.

27

Akpek is waiting for Tomas at the dogsled. Akpek has no catch, but his eyes widen with delight as he helps Tomas haul his seal out of the water.

The huskies bring them back to the igloo. Mamayauk calls everyone out to greet them. Even Ekalukpik crawls out of the igloo!

Mamayauk grabs Tomas and they rub noses.

"It is wonderful!" she says, admiring the seal.

Mamayauk and the other women prepare the seal meat. When it is all cut up, Ekalukpik pulls Tomas aside. He whispers in Tomas's ear what he must do next.

Tomas collects all of the seal bones and packs them in a bag. Then he rides the dogsled back to the edge of the ice. He dumps the bones back in the water, out of respect for the seal. Ekalukpik told him to do this to assure successful hunts to come.

Tomas pulls his coat closer around him to protect him from a cold gust of wind.

"What do you have your coat on for?" Emma asks.

"It's hot in here," adds Kevin.

Tomas is surrounded by his friends. He's back at the museum, wearing his jacket.

"I was cold a minute ago." Tomas is dazed.

"Well, take it off. We're not leaving yet! We still have more to see," says Lucy.

He joins the others as they continue through the exhibit. Now he can't wait to go camping with his scout troop. He wants to teach them a lesson or two about survival.

POLAR ESKIMO
THE NORTHERNMOST PEOPLE OF THE WORLD

31

About the Inuit

The Arctic may have seemed like a barren wasteland with its miles of snow and months without sun. But the Inuit (also referred to as Eskimos) knew it was a land full of life. "Inuit" is a name that means "the people."

About ten thousand years ago, much of the earth's water was frozen in glaciers, and a "land bridge," named the Bering Strait, connected Asia to North America. It is believed that the Inuit came to North America four thousand years ago over this land bridge. The earliest Inuit settled on the shores of Alaska, Canada, and Greenland. Here, in these arctic and subarctic regions, Inuit culture developed and flourished. It remained undisturbed until the nineteenth century.

In the biting cold environment of the Arctic, where temperatures often fall to 60 degrees below zero, survival was most important. Therefore, hunting was a vital part of Inuit life. They hunted whales, seals, walruses, caribou, fish, and birds. These animals provided the Inuit with everything they needed. They made parkas, mittens, boots, tents, and dolls from seal or caribou skin. Boats and lines were made from the skins of seal and walrus. Needles and ornaments were made from walrus tusks. Oil for lamps and medicine was made from blubber. The Inuit had a deep respect for the animals they hunted, because they knew that without them, they could not survive.

The term "igloo" technically means any type of house. While round igloos made out of snow are probably the most recognizable Inuit homes, most tribes used them as temporary shelters while on hunting trips, but made houses out of wood, stone, earth, or bone covered with caribou or seal skins. In the summers, many Inuit lived in coastal regions in skin tents.

Only in northern Canada were snow igloos (or igluvigaks) used as shelters through the whole winter. The snow blocks were stacked in an ascending upward spiral on top of each other, and a covering of snow on the outside sealed up all the cracks. In the wind, the snow blocks settled and became strong as cement.

Inuit culture was filled with storytelling and art. Family was central and the Inuit lived in large extended family groups. Their settlements ranged from 30-60 people. Members of a community each played an important part in activities, such as hunting and home life, to ensure survival in the harsh land of ice and snow.

Today, Inuit live in a modern society and wear western clothes. But at times of ceremony they dress in their fancy, traditional clothing. Inuit culture remains very much alive, therefore, in the traditions of the native peoples of Russia, Alaska, Canada, and Greenland.

Glossary

Arctic Circle: area around the North Pole and the Arctic Ocean, at 66 degree North latitude, characterized by its extremely cold temperatures

caribou: type of large deer found in tundra habitats, related to Eurasian reindeer

harpoon: long, spearlike weapon with a bone or ivory tip attached to a long line, and used to hunt walruses, whales, and seals

ice floe: large piece of sea ice floating in the ocean

insulation: protection from outside elements

kayak: covered sealskin boat with a hole in the top for one or more rider(s), used primarily on hunting expeditions

Northern Lights: lights that flicker or streak through the sky caused by electric particles from the sun. Also known as the aurora borealis

parka: heavy jacket with a hood for extra warmth, originally of caribou or polar bear fur

tundra: treeless land in the arctic zone where soil beneath the surface is permanently frozen